Rare & Blue

Finding Nature's Treasures

Constance Van Hoven

Illustrated by Alan Marks

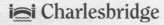 Charlesbridge

How do you find nature's treasures,
both rare and blue? Set off on a hunt!

To find silvery blue,
circle a patch of lupine.
Keep your eyes close to the ground . . .

Whee! Karner blue butterflies!

Tiny Karner blue butterflies collect in fields of wild lupine because the Karner blue caterpillar's only food is lupine leaves. Unfortunately, much lupine habitat has been replaced by farms, houses, and roads. Karner blues still exist, though, in seven US states.

To find iridescent blue,
rumble through the desert to an oasis pond.
Peer beneath algae clumps . . .

Over here, over there, Quitobaquito pupfish!

Male pupfish turn blue to attract a mate and once swam in ponds across the southwestern United States and Mexico. Because water has been pumped out of the ground to supply water for drinking and for growing crops, many pupfish ponds have dried up. Today, the Quitobaquito species live in one pond in the Arizona desert, in small springs in Mexico, and in aquariums.

To find electric blue,
hike into a tall forest.
Listen for *zray, zray, zray, zreeeee* . . .

Hello up there, cerulean warbler!

Male cerulean warblers are said to wear the sky on their back. It can be difficult to see their colorful feathers, though, because they nest and forage at the top of trees. These birds are on the decline due to old forest destruction in North America for mining and logging, and in South America for coffee growing.

To find sapphire blue,
ply coastal waters.
Haul traps from dawn to dusk . . .

Well, look at that. A blue lobster!

Lobsters that live in the North Atlantic ocean are most
commonly greenish brown, but on rare occasions,
they can be blue. Biologists guess that the blue color
variation occurs in one in every two million lobsters.
This is why catching a blue lobster is believed to bring
good luck to a lobster boat!

To find midnight blue,
slog through flatwoods.
Inspect abandoned tortoise burrows . . .

Surprise, eastern indigo snake!

Eastern indigo snakes have blue–black bodies with smooth scales that glisten in sunlight. They like to lay their eggs in burrows dug by gopher tortoises. Both tortoises and snakes need large amounts of undisturbed land to survive. As human population grows, the snakes' habitat in the southeastern United States is being replaced with buildings and roads.

To find steely blue,
go to where bison roam.
Cast your eyes across an endless field . . .

Aha! Big bluestem prairie grass!

*In the summer, big bluestem takes on a blue-green cast,
making swaths of this waving grass look like an ocean.
During the 1800s in central North America, millions of acres
of tallgrass prairie were turned into farm fields or pasture.
Today, it is one of the rarest and most endangered ecosystems.*

To find pearly blue,
kayak an icy bay.
Scan the shoreline for a rubbing tree . . .

Where are you, blue black bear?

American black bears can be black, brown, cinnamon, blond, white, and yes, even blue. Blue bears exist only in southeastern Alaska. They have a deep blue-black undercoat, while outer hairs are long and white with silver tips. The rare blue coloration may have developed long ago as camouflage for living near ice fields.

To find turquoise blue,
skim over the ocean.
Survey waves for spouts and flukes . . .

Ahoy, blue whales!

Blue whales look gray above water, but underwater
they appear turquoise. They are the largest animals
on Earth and are threatened by climate change, toxins
in the ocean, and collisions with ships. Eight to nine
thousand blue whales likely exist worldwide.

Finally, to find breathtaking, brilliant blue,
BLAST into space.
Gaze out the window . . .

Behold the jewel of the universe.
planet Earth, our home and home to
nature's treasures rare and blue.

Earth is called the blue planet because so much of its surface is covered in water. No other planet has yet been found with the same combination of water, air, and sunlight, which is necessary to support life as we know it. This makes Earth the rarest blue wonder of all.

Categories of Species

rare: not often found or seen; uncommon

naturally rare: when there are only a few members of a species to begin with

threatened: when the members of a species are likely to become endangered within the foreseeable future throughout all or a significant portion of their range

endangered: when the members of a species are so few or declining so quickly that the species may soon not exist at all

extinct: when the members of a species are officially all gone

Words to Know

camouflage: to hide by disguise, blending in to the environment; many animals use camouflage as a defense against predators.

canopy: the uppermost spreading branches of trees forming a continuous layer of leaves

cerulean: resembling the blue of the sky

flatwoods: dry, low-lying timberland with lots of pine trees

forage: to search for food

genetics: the study of heredity or how living things pass on characteristics

habitat: the place where a plant or animal normally lives and grows

indigo: a color between blue and purple

pine barren: an open sunny landscape with grassy patches between stands of pitch pine and scrub oak

rubbing tree: a tree that bears rub against to mark their presence for other bears; bears tend to travel the same routes every day along a beach or streambed, often rubbing on the same trees and leaving bits of hair attached to the bark.

More Rare and Blue Facts

Karner Blue Butterfly: *Lycaeides melissa samuelis*

Size: Wingspan about one inch

Habitat: Pine barrens of North America

Status: On the US Fish and Wildlife Service Endangered Species List since 1992. Today Karner blues are making a comeback in several states due to reintroduction programs.

Where to look: Necedah National Wildlife Refuge, Wisconsin, in early May and August

Quitobaquito or Rio Sonoyta Pupfish: *Cyprinodon eremus*

Size: About two inches long

Habitat: Desert ponds, marshes, and springs of North America

Status: On the US Fish and Wildlife Service Endangered Species List since 1986

Where to look: Organ Pipe Cactus National Monument, Arizona, from April through August

Cerulean Warbler: *Setophaga cerulea*
Size: About four inches long, with eight-inch wingspan
Habitat: Mature forests with high canopy, North America and South America
Status: A species of concern, under consideration for threatened status
Where to look: Monongahela National Forest Area, West Virginia from May to August

North American Lobster: *Homarus americanus*
Size: A lobster continues to grow throughout its life; an average adult weighs three pounds. The largest lobster on record weighed forty-four pounds and was almost four feet long.
Habitat: On the Atlantic Ocean floor from Canada to North Carolina
Status: Blue lobsters are naturally rare. Even rarer are lobsters with shells that are yellow, spotted orange and black, white, or bright red (before being cooked). While commonly colored brownish-green lobsters are widespread in the waters off northern New England, there is concern that they are not thriving farther south, perhaps because waters are warmer than they used to be.
Where to look: The New England Aquarium in Boston, Massachusetts, has a live blue lobster.

Eastern Indigo Snake: *Drymarchon couperi*
Size: Longest snake in North America, up to nine feet long
Habitat: Pine flatwoods, forested sand hills, swamps, and canals in Georgia and Florida
Status: On the US Fish and Wildlife Service Endangered Species List since 1978; classified as threatened
Where to look: Okefenokee National Wildlife Refuge, Georgia

Big Bluestem Grass: *Andropogon gerardii*
Size: Grows three to ten feet tall
Habitat: Dominant grass of the tallgrass prairie that once covered Central North America from Canada to Mexico
Status: Only 4 percent of the original native tallgrass prairie remains.
Where to look: The Tallgrass Prairie National Preserve, Kansas

Blue Bear: *Ursus americanus emmonsii* (this subspecies of American black bear may also be referred to as a glacier bear)
Size: 150 to 300 pounds
Habitat: Forests of Alaska
Status: Naturally rare. Although the overall black bear population is increasing, bears with the blue color variation may be decreasing.
Where to look: Russell Fjord Wilderness near Hubbard Glacier, Alaska

Blue Whale: *Balaenoptera musculus*
Size: 70 to 100 feet long, weighing up to 200 tons
Habitat: Deep ocean water, worldwide except the Arctic
Status: On the Endangered Species List since 1970, but their population is increasing.
Where to look: Monterey Bay National Marine Sanctuary, California

Planet Earth
Size: The fifth largest planet in the solar system, with an equatorial diameter of 7,917.5 miles
Status: Naturally rare
Where to learn more: Visit exhibits at the Kennedy Space Center near Orlando, Florida.

Selected Bibliography

"Blue Whales: The Largest Animal on Earth." The Marine Mammal Center. www.marinemammalcenter. org/education/marine-mammal-information/cetaceans/blue-whale.html

Brower, Kenneth. "Still Blue." *National Geographic*, March 2009: 134–152.

"Cerulean Warbler Life History." The Cornell Lab of Ornithology, *All About Birds*. https://www. allaboutbirds.org/guide/Cerulean_Warbler/lifehistory

"Last Stand of the Tallgrass Prairie." National Park Service, Tallgrass Prairie National Preserve, Kansas. https://www.nps.gov/tapr/index.htm

DeCosta-Klipa, Nik. "Orange, Yellow, Blue, and Even 'Halloween': The Rarest Lobster Colors, Explained." Boston.com, September 13, 2017. www.boston.com/news/animals/2017/09/13/the-rarest-lobster-colors-explained

Drake, Nadia. "Beyond the Blue Marble." *National Geographic*, March 2018: 68–77.

"Eastern Indigo Snake Fact Sheet." US Fish and Wildlife Service, Panama City (Florida) Field Office. https://www.fws.gov/panamacity/resources/EasternIndigoSnakeFactSheet.pdf

Gray, Susan H. *Road to Recovery: Karner Blue Butterfly*. Ann Arbor: Cherry Lake Publishing, 2008.

"Karner Blue Butterfly Fact Sheet." US Fish and Wildlife Service, Midwest Region, Endangered Species. https://www.fws.gov/midwest/endangered/insects/kbb/index.html

Miller, Matthew L. "When Is a Black Bear Actually a Blue Bear?" Cool Green Science blog, Nature.org, February 7, 2017. https://blog.nature.org/science/2017/02/07/when-black-bear-actually-blue-bear-color-phases-grizzly-identification/

Powell, Robert, Roger Conant, and Joseph T. Collins. *Peterson Field Guide to Reptiles and Amphibians of Eastern and Central North America*. 4th ed. Boston: Houghton Mifflin Harcourt, 2016.

"Quitobaquito and Rio Sonoyta Conservation Projects." Arizona-Sonora Desert Museum. www.desertmuseum.org/center/quitobaquito.php

Into the Wild Blue Yonder

For information and tips on responsibly viewing wildlife and natural wonders, visit your own state's Department of Natural Resources, Fish and Wildlife Service, or Wildlife and Parks websites. Here's an example of Montana's Fish, Wildlife and Parks website: www.fwp.mt.gov/recreation/ethics/.

"In the vastness of space sits beautiful, blue planet Earth, the only place that can provide everything we need. Let's be good stewards of our only home."

—Karen Nyberg, NASA Astronaut

For my true blue family, especially Greg—C. V. H.

For Joyce Tong, and to the memory of Edwin Tong— my good neighbors—A. M.

Text copyright © 2020 by Constance Van Hoven
Illustrations copyright © 2020 by Alan Marks
All rights reserved, including the right of reproduction in whole or in part in any form.
Charlesbridge and colophon are registered trademarks of Charlesbridge Publishing, Inc.

At the time of publication, any URLs printed in this book were accurate and active. Charlesbridge, the author, and the illustrator are not responsible for the content or accessibility of any URL.

Published by Charlesbridge
85 Main Street
Watertown, MA 02472
(617) 926-0329
www.charlesbridge.com

Library of Congress Cataloging-in-Publication Data
Names: Van Hoven, Constance, author. | Marks, Alan, 1957- illustrator.
Title: Rare and blue: finding nature's treasures / Constance Van Hoven; illustrated by Alan Marks.
Description: Watertown, MA: Charlesbridge, [2020] | Includes bibliographical references. |
Identifiers: LCCN 2019014252 (print) | LCCN 2019018038 (ebook) | ISBN 9781632898494 (ebook) | ISBN 9781632898500 (e-book pdf) | ISBN 9781623540975 (reinforced for library use)
Subjects: LCSH: Rare animals—Juvenile literature. | Blue—Juvenile literature.
Classification: LCC QL83 (ebook) | LCC QL83 .V36 2020 (print) | DDC 591.68—dc23
LC record available at https://lccn.loc.gov/2019014252

Printed in China
(hc) 10 9 8 7 6 5 4 3 2 1

Illustrations done in watercolor inks on Fabriano 5 paper
Display type set in Blue Liquid by Creativeqube Design
Text type set in Blauth by Sofia Mohr
Color separations by Colourscan Print Co Pte Ltd, Singapore
Printed by 1010 Printing International Limited in Huizhou, Guangdong, China
Production supervision by Brian G. Walker
Designed by Diane M. Earley